From Sorrow to the Stars

Adeen Azam

BOOK HOME

From Sorrow to the Stars

Written by: Adeen Azam

Cover art by: Adeen Azam

Cover design by: Muhammad Ahsun Gull

'From Sorrow to the Stars' copyright © 2020 Adeen Azam

All rights reserved

adeenazam205@gmail.com

Arranged by: Rana Abdul Rehman

Produced by: M. Sarwar

Composed by: M. Anwar

Printed in Pakistan by: H. H. Printers Lahore

Published by: Book Home Publishers Lahore

Price:

www.bookhomepublishers.com

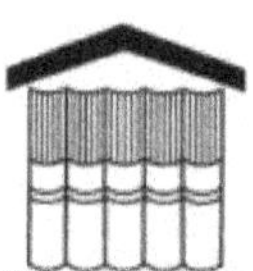

BOOK HOME
Book Street 46-Mozang Road Lahore
Ph: 042-37231518, 37245072
E-mail:bookhomepublishers@gmail.com-bookhome_1@yahoo.com
www.bookhomepublishers.com

About the Book

Let's skip the part where I could've told you that this book is about how to traverse from hopeless melancholy to the realm of stars. This book is about what we decide to happen between you and me, whatever will happen when you draw yourself up from the depths of everything that aches to everything that's glorious. We will create a place among the stars and soar above the sorrows, grief, melancholia, heartbreak, rage, emptiness, numbness or whatever you label your weakness to be.

This book isn't about the people you've loved or the people you never got to have. It is about how you and I managed to climb over all the obstacles and all the heartbreak and managed to create a sanctuary here. A sanctuary where we read a few pages for you, that might mean something to you one day.

And for me to write and pour my love into words so they might comfort you like warm sunlight on a cold winter day.

This book is about us. How we loved in our own ways. How we didn't give up and tried in the ways we knew. How we had dreams and nightmares and despite living in reality. How the both of us exist in our own beautiful ways. How we broke tragically and how we healed gracefully.

This book isn't a mere collection of poetry and prose. It is my hand that held a pen wrote on a crowd ness of papers I might find solace between these pages. It is my body that sat restless in a chair, awaiting relief which was found in writing a meaningful poem.

This book is about the words. How they fit together and give a meaning. A life to a sentence. How they undress emotions, tearing away their veneers.

It's about you and I struggling, hand in hand, trying to find a beacon of light to illuminate our paths in the endless dark. And I hope you might find that luminance, that solace, that comfort in this random book resting on a bookshelf and may your eyes crave to read the words which were penned by my love for your contentment.

Introduction

If I just put together the pieces of my heart and burrow the past, where I broke my self. Is when I create something so colossal out of some mere words. What we call poetry.

And what my fractured heart wrings out here, in the pages of my book, is nothing but the death of it.

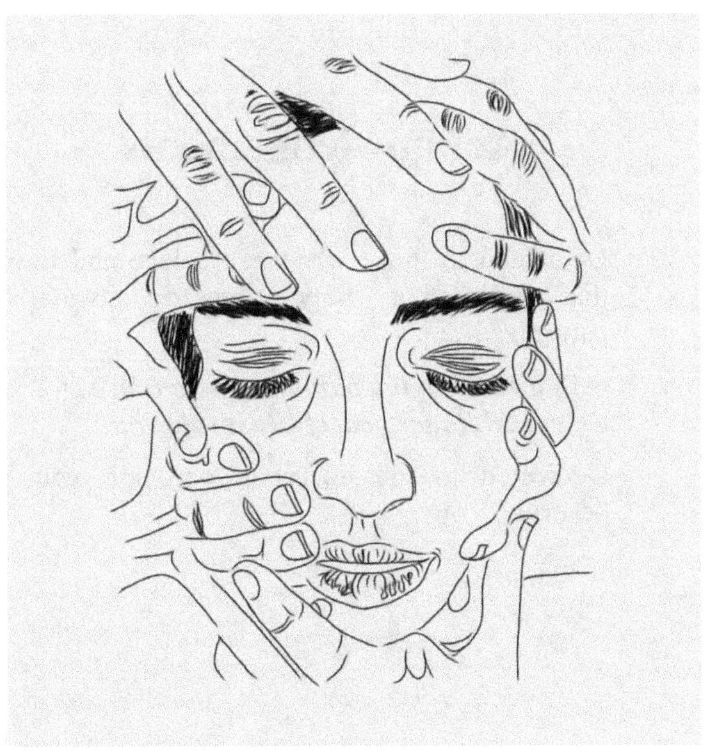

Acknowledgements

Dedicated to those who seek solace and to that little big hope they've always patronized

Dedicated to the pains you've cured Yet still linger peacefully inside you

Dedicated to the upcoming strength you deserve.

Contents

Words of Happiness

Write about happiness I told myself

Write about the nostalgia and the fantasies you have

Write about how you always wanted the sunlight unwind inside every atom of you

Write about how your heart tickles when something is happening, you always wanted to live for

Write how ethereal it felt when you used to melt down whenever someone took you in their embrace

Write about it

Write every second of it

Write about when you smiled long enough to make your cheeks ache even for a vain cause

Write about how you didn't want to blink

Whenever you were glad because you didn't want to skip a single sight for these sour eyes yet also flickered in haste to know if it was all real or just some false fad

Write about how you could not contain

Yourself whenever you felt more beautiful than you wanted to write about it all

Just don't remind these pages the sorrow what used to be before these moments and don't torture yourself with the forged hopelessness your valor might have after them.

The Insane Talk

I'm among the insane

And I hear them talking

They are saying words

They have been clutching to their tongues

They are screaming with their lips sutured

The darkness behind their eyes

Tormenting their very existences

They refuse to feed themselves

They know not what good will it bring to them.

I'm among the insane

They don't demand any laurels

To adorn their heads

Or some throne to settle on.

I'm among the insane

They've been victims of heartache

They've been broken at every breath

They've suffocated for solace

They've starved for some beauty to this reality.

I'm among the insane

And I'd dare not want to call myself lucid and sane

Because sane means to be quiet unless you're asked to speak

Sane means feeling to the hems and haws of their wands

Sane means having a spell cast on you

Sane means puppetry

And I demur to be another dupe

Though we might be far off better drowning in

Some illusion than struggling to swim in our own heads.

Loving the Right One

And I can't help it but find it dazzling how much you can love someone who is not for you but just imagine how much you'll love the person who is actually meant for you. It's odd how you are hurting and there is a person in existence who doesn't even know you, hasn't even met you but still is thinking about and absolutely in love with the idea of loving you. There's a person who hasn't even seen you but is already adoring the fact that you're in love with her too. It's sad but it's pleasing. There's so much to see in a person besides their smile, their eyes, besides traces of yourself in them. You have to look for them in themselves.

For they will definitely be loving you for you and not what you pretend to be for the sake of acceptance in this unlovely world.

My Heart, a Boon and a Blasphemy

Consider it a boon or blasphemy but I never treated this heart of mine something I could have any word on. Just like how I let it beat, I let it love. I let it strive and thrive for what it wants. I let it break and heal spontaneously, unspontaneously. This heart. It still beats where I don't want it to. It still loves when I hate it to. And I wouldn't have known how it feels to own something so dynamic, so certain let alone even uncertain of what it wants. I would never know how to own it or let someone own it. I'd rather have it as a keeper of its own. For I could never control something that beats, lives and loves so beautifully willing and lucid.

Happiness That Heals

Happiness.

Happiness is like the sunrise and sunset.

Mesmerizing.

They can be just

Mere moments that Occur often.

They don't last Long.

But as long as

They do,

We're left with

Our eyes wide

Upon wondering.

How can something,

Be so beautiful and blinding.

Journey From the Past to Now

When I tell you about
Myself
When I tell you, I have healed from my Past.
Doesn't mean
It doesn't hurt anymore.
Doesn't mean
I never cry for it.
Doesn't mean
I have let gone of it.

It just means
This history of mine
Doesn't let me lose hope
For the life to come as
Much as I had lost it
Before
It doesn't demand pain
Anymore when I thought
That's all I ever deserved.

And this is what a
Beautiful.
Now asks for.

Things I'm Ready For

Don't ask me if

I'm hurting

Or if I've ever

Been in love.

Just know

I've survived

Whatever I've

Been through.

And here I am

Ready to love

Ready to break

Alive to die.

The End of Everything

The sky was in

Spitting distance

As if I didn't need the

Horizon to touch

It

While you were

Sitting beside me

Yet too far away

But my love for

You took me afar

From the seven

Skies as I

Watched the world

Stop chasing me

And I knew this

Was the end of

Everything.

Realizations

You do not stay at one place. With one Person.

Because I know you're afraid you think

You'll miss something, someone better

Somewhere else.

Because you can't do better.

You think you are not worthy and able of what you hold dear, where you are with someone good enough.

Maybe, you were made felt like that by your Past.

That past, you're still not come over yet.

I guess it's not your fault, nor is it mine. Whose it is then? We don't know. It just happens and we can't do anything about it but survive it.

We have to do it to realize why people

Leave telling us that we deserve better so it

Hurts better. We have to realize that

Moments are not going to happen how we want them to. And some people always won't make a difference like we want them to.

The Beauties Within You

Isn't it beautiful
To live,
To live somewhere
You feel like you don't even belong
Yet you stay
And make it worth your while.
You make those stars want to fall and dwell
Beside you
You let your sun dawn and moon dusk.
You make a beautiful stay even in a not so
Tenantable dust
You remain alive even among the lifeless.
And believe me
This life in you
Is contagious.
Everything is not so dead after all
With being bestowed by your essence
With you still breathing the air
With you still loving despite the hurt
With you still healing despite the agony of it
With you still being there despite every reason not to.

Fate for Faith

But the person

Who truly loves you, won't demand an invitation to visit your pain and try to deaden

It.

They won't ask

You, for your

Trust.

They will simply give you their own and then secure

yours.

Just like that.

By words. By

Gentle gestures.

By their great

Gravity.

To Writers of Forevers

There will arrive a moment when
You would no longer want to
Poeticize the pain, you would no
Longer want to write with respect to
The beauty of the person who
Refuses loving you
Within that moment, you'll realize no
Words could ever make vivid even a
Quarter of their intricacy and
Exquisiteness.
It will be a helpless time for you
But it's all you'll be needing
You just need to have faith in your
Feelings instead of some words
And you'll know what you have to
And your pen will put the right words
On another paper
That now believes (forever is a word used by people who've just lost their tracks of times).
To those who think they can't write on love anymore.
Have patience. Worry not.
All the empty pages in your diary know the truth
Behind you not being able to give them some ink.

Lost love

I was lost for love
I was lost in love
I lost to love
I lost from love
I loved and I lost.

Love was lost for me
Love was lost in me
Somewhere for someone.

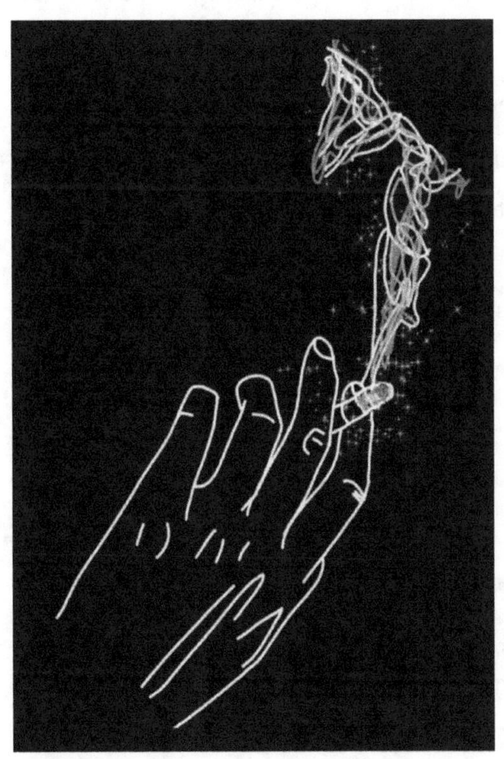

Melancholy and Me

Stop being so weak

And yellow-bellied you're better than that she tells me

I look at her glassy-eyed

Shot to pieces

Offering my back to the pain in my

Mother's eyes

Breaking my neck as I wilt my head once

Again for my father

Carving a grin to my lover who has left 31

Times and returned once more for another

Piece of my heart

Sewing the wounds on my body

Everywhere but on my heart and soul

Putting on this season's facade on my lips

And ears

Pouring myself some heavy drink into my mouth with some hard pills to swallow, kneeling down facing the wall God is here, Falling on the bathroom floor half dead, and lay there in tears until my eyes burn, and the air stings

Walking out like harlequin ready to kiss the
Ones I need to kill.
If this is weak.

Then indeed, I'm so weak.
Melancholy knows I'm better than her.

Expires: now
Love pills
are more than one for quick results
Love pills
Love pills
Love pills
Love pills
Made in heartbreak™
Made in heartbreak™
Made in heartbreak™
Made in heartbreak™
Made in heartbreak™

The Loving Before Losing

The stars ensconce in the haze

The moon cowers behind the clouds

You disappear in the night while I wait for the sun to ape up, the blue to glow and rouge.

It's an another day for loving you after

Spending another night, afraid of losing You.

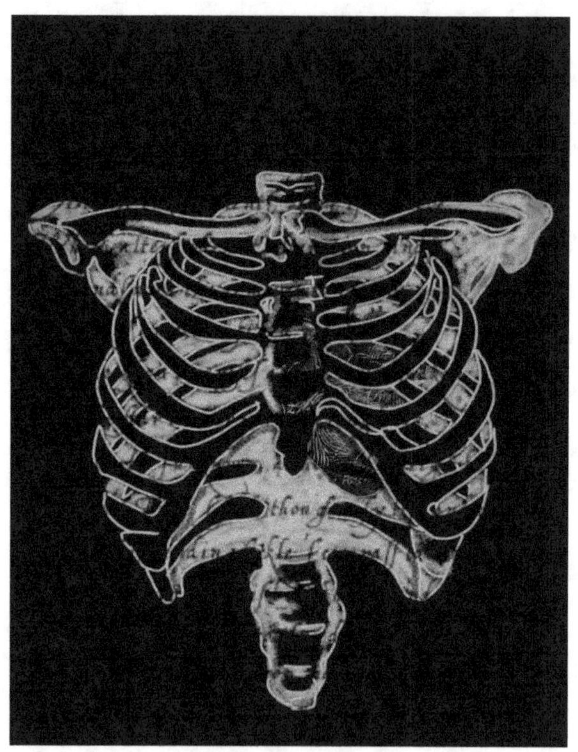

A Better Healing

You're going to go through this same hurt again but the next time, you'll heal

differently.

And if you feel like the hurt is

Worse, then know, the healing is surely going to be better.

Things we Choose to be

The things we do to

Benumb the pain

The words we say to smother the love

It's not who we are

It's just what we choose

To be.

Healing the Invited Aches

And unfortunately, I've learnt

The world will profane this tender soul of yours. They won't stop until every inch of your skin by this soul crisps dry to wither.

Just to feel better about their own flesh.

I've learnt.

It's better to live.

Better to seem

Soulless with a heart of iron.

Not to be an uncertain saint but less of an

Inevitable sinner.

Not just to shun uninvited pains but to heal, what

Of them is already there.

Self Help

I've been hostile to my skin for so long
I've forgotten how it truly feels to live in
Something intact and unscathed
It feels skewed, concave and convex at
Places, where once twinges had built their
Homes but left in the search of a better
Place later leaving behind traces of their
Existence
Now, I carry this anxious skin, afraid to meet
Other skins because it has had
Enough. Another touch will shatter its
Delicate pieces holding onto each other.
I'm afraid, afraid of my lurid self and afraid
How the world would never accept this gore
So, I want those eyes to be blind that see
My skin, I want those fingers benumbed
Because this surface is no longer holy, it's
Polluted with timeless pain that I rouse

Even when I no longer have the grit to ruin

What's left of me

So forgive me, if you're still unfamiliar with

My leathery coat

I've been trying to own it and I want no

Other to meddle as what I have destroyed   Is meant to be revived by me for there's no better destruction and healing one can do to one's self.

How I'll Survive my Tomorrow

I'd say memories gave

Me some spectacular

Visions and phantasms all of their own.

To call my own but with

Most here came the

Abjured pain I can't carry

Yet don't want them dust

So that I remember how

To endure the life to come

And how I've

Survived the yesterdays and tomorrows I've had.

Explosion of a Heart Break

It felt like explosions among those ribs

Pain flowing restlessly in my torso

That burning sensation that made you weak in

Every way

Those incessant pangs in the head

They were those stinging thoughts you tried to

Avoid

It made every muscle, every vein ache

There was utter silence in that body

Silence nourished in every nerve

Words could have failed to describe the pain that misery
You could feel your blood flow faster

You could hear your heart pounding in your ears

You could feel a scream building up inside

You could feel your flesh acclimatize

You felt the need to clench your fists until your

Knuckles ache

You could feel your eyes burning, your body turning warmer and hands getting colder.

You start sweating in cold.

You clench your jaws hoping that tightening yourself would make you feel stronger.

How tears escape from your eyes as you scream.

His name with all the strength you have left. And then, I knew. That is what the explosion of a heart break sounds like.

Jaan se Jahan

The word 'jaan' reels out of his mouth on a thread entwined with a warm shawl made up of jaan aforesaid a million times.

And as I swathe that shawl around me from head to toe. The words'meri jaan'meaning 'my life'

Touch me and smash my winter skin to smithereens with their warmth. And my coal bones still keep all his love intact .

And I just stand in front of him,with my heart burning beneath all that glass skin and coal bones,igniting the butterflies in my chest. As they sky out of my lips and I whisper 'I love you too meri jaan'

And I realize he has a beautiful choice of words. The way he weaves them together. It's beautiful. How can someone not love him. How can someone not want to have a taste of this clement sweetness plastered on his tongue. And such a love smeared on his lips. I can only wonder…..

Life for Me

I'm lost in the silence

Wrapped in this crowd of words, wandering

In the truth why the world revolves to come

Back at the same site but has quite

Changes with every spin yet

I'm stuck whether to feel the bliss of nostalgia to

These scars

I'm dazed, bewildered whether to live

The not occurring moments in my head or study

What's happening timelessly

For me, a maze,

A life

It's neither about appearing at the

Beginning nor the want to disappear at

Some point

It's neither about starting the journey and

Wanting to change it

It's about the struggle in between to

Fathom what you need, not want
It's about the eagerness to no longer feel
Entrapped
It's about having hope deep down that
'You'll grow whatever you go through.

How Crying is not a Weakness

Cry my darling
Before these eyes refuse to walk
Out the melancholy
Shed those tears now
Before they demur to not let it
Thrive inside you
Don't limit the rivers in there
Before they promise the pain a
Timeless stay, a deluge
Before it's all that there is
Let your eyes bleed
Let every ounce sweep away the
Filth of those sore moments
Let it all out
Uncage too what doesn't belong in
Cry, whimper, and sob
It won't be ingratitude,
It'd be relief
Not some weakness
But an invitation to the might
So ready to barge in.

Growing up to Love

When you told me

To let you go and

Move on with

Someone better

I know you meant

To tell me to

Grow up for

Someone who is

Worthy of my love.

People who Deserve You

The only people who

Deserve you are those who

Make you wade through

Yourself more. They will

Make you learn your worth, awake your might.

Instead of making yourself

Forget the realities, the

Truths to you, your past, Your

forging.

What Love Does to You

Love like the

Fire

You'll burn

Love like the

Waves

You'll drown

Love like you do

You'll break

We all love,

We all hurt.

But we stay ,not for the hurt but the love.

Old Wounds

Sometimes, some scars lay

Themselves open and bleed again

When they are prevailed upon by what once conjured and kindled them.

And such scars never stop

Hurting even when they seem healed, look exquisite. Their quiet presence hurts

More than any else's.

Privileges of Loving

The sky tells me if I get

Any closer to you, I

Won't have the privilege

To live or breathe but

Just love and be

Breathless by the

Beauty of it. And never say die to anything that comes with
it. Even that

Silence. The pain.

The Truth of Endings

God says

The end makes the truths win

And if you're still at loss in this life alike an

Endless spin

Then it's not the end, there's still hope

Like before every finis, there has been

And to come to a laugher

You have to alter the lines on your hand

Like a man

Runs on the blood same of his kin

And indeed the end

For the aftermath of your sacrifices

Your devotions

Victory

Despite your every sin

And every pounding peril

Win will itself chase you as long as you

Keep the will.

The Tears Love Sheds

If I could scare up all those tears I had shed for you.

If not the world, I would drown.

If not me, then the world will soon.

That Feeling in Your Pith

Through that epoch, I always

Considered you euphoric. Now, that

I'm awake and sober. You are just

The tears that left my eyes yet the few that

Stayed on the rims just like how you

Left my life yet stayed in my heart

And these late memories. Which makes me thinks of if you
still believe these feelings, in your pith, that keep reeling.

A Woman, a Weak Vigor

I'm shoved into a wall

Told that I'm just a lump of blunders.

I'm a prey to a leather belt in the hands of a so called

Man.

My skin is a canvas for having bruises painted all over

It.

Every strand of my hair is threatened to ache until each one
of them falls out.

My eyes are mere portraits of pain

My soul itself is an abyss

Where my tolerance burns.

My arms are my armors while my stomach is a habit

Of dearth and my mouth is a drought.

I starve for happiness and healing

And yet I'm still meant to give life

For I'm just a puppet of a voice capable of waking up

The dead.

I'm a tear made of fears and empty nostalgia

I'm dragged out of my solace by my accepting

Buoyancy.

I'm a slave of my frail body

That is the butcher of everything it could be more than a
Woman.

My Presence in my Poems

And I'd wait to hurt to know that I ever healed & I'll

Have to appear in my poems to know that I ever

Disappeared while loving you. I have to be in blues to

Know that I once loved in red & might still do. Loving

You is heavier than the hurting but I do it anyway

Because I have to, I need to. I wait to empty myself in

You & let you know that my hollow is full of

Something & anythings & of somebodys &

Anybodys. Gloom is cascading out of my remains but   I'll
Create radiant glee for you anyway. Yes, I can't wait

To allure you in the pursuits of love & let you know

How extreme it can be and how people like me are

Always willing to give away anything to their beloved

Ones even when they have nothing left

Anymore. They'll still find you in their dark chasms and
Find love within to give because they're never just

Running out of it. I don't know how longer will the love

& wait last but it will be longed forever. Forever exists

Only if someone is willing to meet it. I can wait to love

But forever can't. But know this is the kind of love born

That'll defeat entities to win you. I can wait, forever. So, be
my forever.

Romanticizing a Silhouette

You've

Romanticized the

Silhouette of a   Love that barely ever existed.

It's about time

You meet it in

Person. Meet

Yourself. In

This little

Deathless light.

For this untold Darkness.

Meet this love,

That doesn't

Fade. It stays

At all

See for

Yourself. You

Are beautiful, Love.

All the Hurt in me Shall Talk

My scars will tell you

How hurt is endured

They will tell you how deeply they were carved in

The past not knowing I was making a blade sink

In my skin.

My heavy tears will tell you how much silence is

Throbbing in them and now they're tired of falling

From two scorching eyes as if they had an

Essence of the sun in them.

My voice will tell you how hardly it escapes the

Mouth and how badly it wants her plaint to reach

Out to you.

My touch will tell you how it turned too cold after waiting
for so long to be felt.

My heart will tell you how long it has yearned for

The love you'll never give

All this hurt in me will speak someday and you'll

Have to listen.

Damage in Disguise

You were so good at hiding the

Damage you had caused to yourself.

I couldn't tell if your tears tasted sour or sweet

And whether my tears were heavier or yours

I just knew you were hurting and healing the same

Time

Unaware of the fact if it was a blessing or a curse.

To People with Broken Hearts

Your agony is greater than we can ever

Bear and your love is greater than we will ever give.

And if knowing it isn't painfully beautiful then we can't fathom the realities to it.

From people with inert hearts.

My Only Muse

The moon was

Staring back at me

And I could tell he envied you for he could never be my

Only muse.

Feeling of Numbness

That feeling of numbness, I think I finally
Learned how to describe it. It's like wanting to cry but
Also not cry at the same time and trying to make
Yourself expressionless and resistant to everything
Happening around. It's a battle between fighting for
Hope but giving up. Shutting down versus rejecting the
Darkness. Being struck by pain so many times like it
Has become a regular routine and you have almost
Adapted to it. There are different ways to handle it but
It depends on the category of numbness you are
Dealing with. Deep down will you never forget the
Moment where you felt you lost it all. That moment
When nothing feels right. You know life is unfair but
You still try to counter these statements. That feeling of
Hopelessness. Your blood boiling with anger but then
Suddenly it's disappearing. Either your rage tries to
Tame itself or just can't decide whether to explode or

Not. A part of you is happy but at the same time you feel a deep chaos inside you. You can't understand

Which emotion will dominate the others. Will the

Happiness smile, will the sad weep or will the anger explode you just stand there feeling numb.

Knowing what to feel exactly. It's more of a maze, a Confusion.

My kind of numbness is staring outside the window

Not knowing what I'm looking for. Staring up at the

Blank ceiling not knowing what to think of. Looking at My hands not knowing why.

What Words do to Scars

If words are just words

Then scars are just

Scars

If words are just

Feelings

Then scars are just their

Vestiges

If words are just lies

Then scars are just

Thorns of true

Awakenings

If words are just

Voiceless

Then scars are just Hollers.

Lonely Times

I've spent time

Over and

Above alone

But not a

Second I have

Not been

Lonely for you.

The Taste of Poison

You know that moment when
You clench your jaws
And grapple your patience as the pain hits
Your heart is of the size of a loosening
Fist
And your tired eyes try to not contain
Those defeated tears, your eyelids have
Been restraining
It's enough
That moment is enough for you to say
You've had enough
You can let go. Begone.
You don't deserve the pain you are
Always willing to adore so much
Just because it's served in front of you
 Before all else on a delicate plate so
Beautiful like a damn dessert.
I don't know what poison tastes like but
Calling some poison a dessert won't make it any sweeter.

How Art Talks

The canvas spoke.

She told me not to

Paint her with pain but

With colors that

Haven't been born yet.

She says she wants to feel salved and novel just

for once.

Like no other.

Without this hurt.

I've kept for so long.

Without every stroke of misery that I have brushed on every masterpiece of mine.

The day I found out, Art has a voice of its own.

Love and Other Addictions

You ask me why do I keep my myself doped all the damn Time and feed on noxious addictions.

I remain silent while staring into space.

You inquire again if your love doesn't bring me solace, Doesn't make me happy, isn't galore, doesn't dilute my Past pains.

I lower my eyes and stare at the phone's screen for a While.

I sigh and reply.

It keeps me numb form the pain of having you so Close

yet so far.

it's me being happy with the fact that you're millions Of miles away, in what seems like another world.   As I gaze at your face dazed, the signal drops Casually and the call disconnects.

I shut my eyes. And ponder why I want you so close to

Me. Why I want you beside me so bad. I don't know. I

Just want your presence really near me. To have

Your eyes to look into. To fall in love a little more.

But you're just too far. And I'm also kind of afraid to

Get too close. I'm not used to loving closely I've Always loved from a distance, afraid it'll hurt if I get Close. Or I could've left myself even to be with you.

But this distance won't ever make me love you any Less. I'll love you more as long as it's endless. I guess I want to love you little different maybe with My heart not so close-lipped. And that's how addiction are.

You want to leave and have them at the same time.

Grief of Grievances

And I'd grieve with those who

Weren't enough for your love

I'd grieve

With my melancholy

With my brokenness

With my lips knit by silence

With my flawed delicacy

With my restless tongue hoisting a

Horde of emotions

With my eyes collapsing into your

Dreams

With my cold skin containing my

Boiling blood

With the very patience in me

I'd still claim

I love you more and grieve and

Yearn

For all the grievances my

Desperation for your love has to

Offer

I'd still grieve for love

A love not so grief-stricken then

I'd love

For now this is how I grieve.

Sad Odes and You

I've been feeling too much

And here I am

Wired to every emotion unfelt

Here I am

Talking about the love I never had

Here I am

Gracing sad odes with the love I

Could never give

Here I am

Encaged to being unsought

Here I am

Waiting

For the lost

I had never even found

Here I am

For you.

How Am I

How am I…
Like an ocean,
An amalgam of
Calm and chaos.

Silver Bracelet

I was suffocating under a white
Pillow that empty night when I
Heard her sobbing with her
Head buried in the bedding
I tried to help myself out,
Maybe to quieten her before
The light follows her, maybe to
Convince her eyes to fall asleep
Already
But I was too feeble to grieve
With her.
Then suddenly,
I felt drenched and disturbed,
Dressed in some mahogany
It was too dark to feel freed
It was too silent to breathe
A razor-sharp hem gashed the
Warm skin under me

I couldn't make it stop

I was no longer able to feel the

Pulse of the wrist I was curved

Around

I was no longer colder than the

Flesh that I met

I no longer felt like I belonged

Somewhere

I no longer knew if I could be

Secured in home dear to one

I no longer knew if I could have

Better hands to take me off and wear me on

If someone could sense and

Take in the fragile life in me

If I could ever be reckoned with

Love.

• (If unloving you was so facile, I would not even find it worth talking about, right now.)

Pills and Potions

I wake up to an empty sky

A pretty much uncluttered bed

Since I lay like a corpse all night

Sometimes with my eyes open

Sometimes closed

I always find a cold cup of vanilla tea sitting on

The table beside my bed

With some pills and a quarter filled water glass

Pills, the ones to get me through half of the day

Water, enough for me to swallow those magic

Bullets

And I don't wake up to any good morning

I've never had

Maybe because the ones around me

Don't think I could have a good one

 Or maybe because they're afraid

That I could toss the cup of tea on the floor and

Draw shambles in the air

Or shove those pills down their own throats to see if it
makes them feel any different

And gulp those ounces of water as my regimen

To deal with this ailment of tongues that talk too

Much of the wrong words and somber lips that

Spit while they emphasize pique

So within this

The time fades

The locks tremble

And I'm numb enough

To be unaware of another twilight

Another night

I don't want to be alive for

That leads to another day

I wish I ceased to exist the exact moment I knew I

Stayed

My Pain, My Souvenir

And for the world,

And when I say for the world

I draw all the pains of it to

Myself,

 I would still choose to give

Love, give all. The love contrived by pain myself.

I would still keep the pains to Myself.

No matter, how thorny it gets.   How scarred I become. I'd still choose to hold the entire pain.

And bestow all the love from every bit of me.

Because I know.

I know. How much I needed it

And how no one was willing to give.

I know how I wanted someone to take this pain away And how it helped me make a home of my own.

Along with the salvation of love that a pain never forgets To bring as a souvenir.

The Sin of Loving Heart Breaks

So it's a tragedy to find

Brokenness beautiful

It's a sin to romanticize

Heartbreak

It's an agony to count every torn

Pore of your soul

Just to feel blessed with

Whatever you're cursed.

Your Blues Before You

I wonder why did I even love such an

Extremity when I knew our calumny was

Going to meet a bitter end

Why did I fall again and not drown to agonize

Instead

I knew how caustic it is every time to show up

At his door and ending up in his tart bed

Maybe I must've heard him wrong or there

Were some words I should've never said

I was a fool to believe his I love you that he

Never meant

I had begun to preach him and his pretense

His love disappeared and I know very well

Where he went

But I'm not going to chase him anymore,

Every ounce of love regrets why it was ever spent on
someone who'll break it to straighten his

Own bend

I don't know about love but you and your

Blues sure will haunt me until I'm dead.

His Love for Her

"I'll never be her I guess", I shrugged.

You said to me while looking at the starry

Sky, "you're better than her". "It's just that she's

Unforgettable and irreplaceable. I can't feel

That love, I had for her, for anyone else."

I killed my whimper when I heard him talk

About her. Suddenly, I was out of breath. My

Misted eyes gazed at him and lord knows how

Miserable I was. Nothing could hurt me more than listening to my flame talk about his love.

I died a million times in a wink and there's nothing more to it.

Night and Heartaches

As the night falls

Heartache invites me in the usual scuffle

Between

My presence and my past

As the next minute asks if I wasn't in

Love the same in both with you

And insomnia brings me the same

Loneliness as all the beautiful lies I Knew, try to cradle me until I'm all tears and fall asleep.

All He Had To Do, He Did

All he ever did
Was strangle all
The love out of
Me,
Leaving me
Forsaken in the
Love, I still had kept latent. He had left once
Again.

Last Times

I'm writing to you for the last time

I don't have more empty words to say

Because you'll never fathom all this love I had for

You all this time

I'm not going to write about the constellations I

Saw in your eyes

I'm not going to write about your mellow voice and

How chills ran down my back every time I heard it

I'm not going to write about the conversations I

Had with the moon

I'm not going to write about those 3am thoughts I

Had every time I fell asleep thinking about you

I'm not going to write about the times I cried

Myself to sleep and woke up trying to figure out

What did I do to deserve this

I'm not going to write about your hands, your

Hair, the way you walked, the way you drove your hands in
your hair and the way your hands fit Perfectly in mine.

I'm not going to write about your chuckle every time I told you I loved you to the moon and back.

I'm not going to write again.

Well, I hope I don't .

Because it couldn't wreck me more than just to love you with a couple of mere words.

That's all I ever did since I saw you.

Love and Other Havocs

I thought what was there left to write

I couldn't know how to hold her

I didn't know

She was stoned

Swinging her hands in the air recklessly

Flipping her hair again and again

Jolting and pulling her head vitally over and

Over as her legs stumbled

As if she was trying to brush off the bitter

Memories of him

And laughing while tears were streaming

Down her face as she listened to don't

Leave by snake hips and mø

I couldn't think of anything at that moment

But trying to home in on her laugh, hiding

Behind her strands of hair occasionally

And stare how peacefully she shed those

Heavy tears from those big cramped eyes

What had become of me

I thought

What have I become

Who am I

I don't know what's wrong and also what's

Right either

Is this love that I don't know

Or a havoc

I've created.

- (All this love Just to remind,
  You have a heart too.)

- (What is this pandemonium
  You've been trying so hard
  To silence between your
  Lungs.)

- (And it still unsettles you how
  Everything holding you together
  Can always tear you apart Wider.
  And at some point, maybe it will.)

- (The worst place to die is in
  An utopian, a sick fantasy.)

- (May you never have scythe your
  Scars
  Just to revive and relive
  The memory of ecstasy, which
  Invited such sorrow to your skin.
  And piqued this very scar.)

Emptiness and Whiskey Bottles

It's not everyday you get to feel like an empty

Bottle of whiskey. Everyone is so pleased to have

It's not everyday you let people hold you. With

Both unaware there not an ounce of ecstasy left

In you

It's not everyday they don't hold you long enough

To leave you or shatter you

It's not everyday you brew love inside you to make them
stay. To have their lips on you to feel

Wanted.

It's not everyday you don't run out of yourself with

Their gulps and guzzles

It's not everyday someone grabs you too hard to

Let out the pain, grasping them

It's not everyday you're afraid to be poured out

Once too many times

But it's everyday

You are to snub the pain

You are to numb the warm veins

It's everyday

You are to be held

You are to be left cold

It's everyday

You can't get used to the perks of solitude

You can't get used to the tears of having lips on

You.

It's everyday

You feed on what feeds on you

You absorb the pain that doesn't belong to you

It's everyday

You can't get out of your habitude

You can't stop loving what wastes you.

Gratitude for Wrong People

I'm more grateful for the wrong

People in my life than the right ones. Because with no doubt, the wrong ones were too right, at least for once, In the time they had with me.

And the right ones, they were just

Hard to accept and deal with wrongly

Unfortunately. For a time, they

Weren't supposed to go through.

Melancholy and Me (pt.2)

I am closer to you than the blood that flows within.

I am closer to your skin than the clothes that cover you.

I am closer to you than the wind that blows past

You.

I am closer to you than the thoughts that cross your mind.

I am a melancholy, you carry within you

Because, you can't be with me and the

Melancholy you feed every time

You feel every time, you watch me walk past you.

I am the melancholy and you, you darling are the whole cause.

Loneliness, My UnInvited Guest

Loneliness

You were never a stranger, never a

Friend, never a visitor, never something

I could love.

You have always been a fucking

Parasite who I let in for the sake of no

Longer feeling hollow

And I let you be warm in me.

I made the ambience so good for you in

There.

But you.

You always had me walking around in

Some fury

Sitting in some sick relief

Like I had let you burn this sanctuary,

You lived within

Just so you could settle back in some

Warm coffin whenever you wanted to

For the change, you came here for

While I gasped in some grave

Because Maybe you couldn't live with the void in there too and maybe you'd leave at times, reminding me how being left hurts more than what leaves does reminding.

How badly I must miss you no matter how much I don't want to just because you were there you were invited there

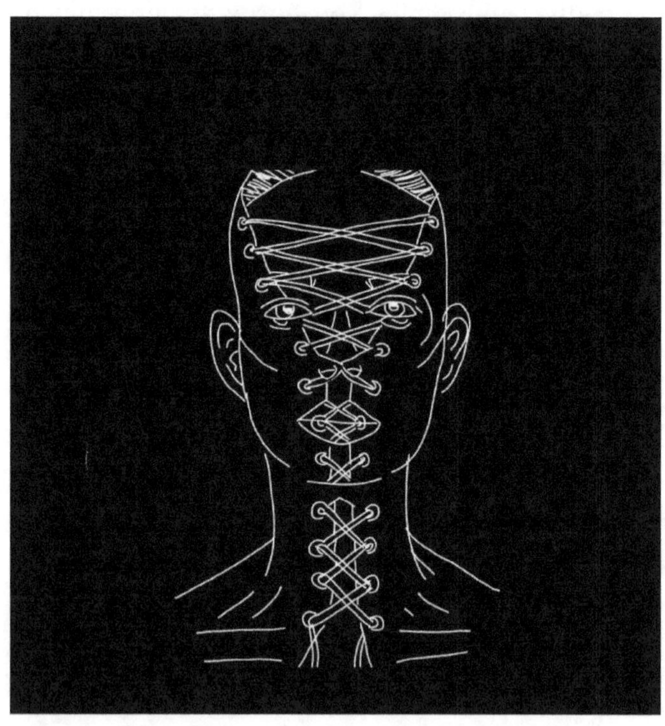

The Sky Knows About Us

I told the sky about you and the clouds have been dancing since then,

seems like they're going to ring the blues when they'll find out about me.

But then the sun marooned and the sky just turned on waterworks as I told them about us.

The sky tore apart, finding out, we're broken.

Inflamed Scars

I could show you my scars from

The inflamed ones to the coldest

But I don't want you asking why they've grown redder since the last

Time you witnessed them.

How Walking Away Hurts

All my life I ate my own pain

Drank all the tears I couldn't let

Stain their cheeks and lips

Silenced myself for them to

Speak

Suffocated myself for them to breathe

Took their scars on my body

Touched their loud voices and

Forgave

Shadowed them in their plight

Saw them in the dark and

Couldn't help but leave my light

Now that I'm overwhelmed and

Prostrate

They tell me to walk away.

The Heart Break

When someone you love leaves

You are not left heart broken

You are left wishing you had been able to listen to their

Voice longer, you had completely heard

Pauses, words, the descent and ascent of

Every cry and say. You wish you had the

Warmth of their voice in your ears longer.

You are left wishing you had been able to get your

Eyes full of them. You wish your eyes had grown

More used to the detail of the map of their face

And body. Their presence. You wait for you to really see
them again. You are left wishing could see what was left to
see. You are left wishing you could begin from where you
left.

You are left wishing you could still feel their scent.

Strong as ever. Feel more of it. And a little more of

It.

You are left wishing you could touch them a little

Longer. The feels of their skin. You could just hold

Their hands.

You are left wishing for long.

You are left wishing they had stayed.

Longer. More.

Not for more memories.

Just stayed for more.

Long enough.

Perhaps, for everything or just me.

Adored Words

They adore those mere words to which they

Can relate but what about those feelings

Unfelt. What about saying words, you don't know what
about those things you never try to look at yet don't want
Them to be left unseen. What about those

Feelings and thoughts you struggle to describe

With some righteous, true words

 You let them

Go away, rove in your head as you find them

Incorrupt and capable of being aforesaid, you find

Them prototypal

Though they are not

And can never be

The same as you convey them

To another. You just let it mean nothing, you forge your
just to let it end itself.

In that moment, you know nothing.

Sometimes to you, it's nothing but tragic.

A Spectacular Love

I used to love it how I was so sure that I'm never going
To get out of this. This love. I'm never letting   him go
Though he doesn't love me. Though it hurts. It hurts to
Have not taken what you've been giving for so long.
Yet if feels worth it. It feels good.
But now instead,
I'm in love with this vain hope that he might be in love
With me.
I'm so in love with it.
That I no longer know if it's him I love.
I'm just too in love with this damn hope of being loved
Not by just anyone but him. Only him.
As my heart has felt now that every heart beats
Different
And his, mine differents were same
I just knew it. Maybe, I knew wrong
But
It still felt worth it. It still feels good. Like it makes me
worthier of myself, makes myself

Paradoxical for this utopia past such hope.

So powerful and awakening at the time.

How spectacular this love is. And I feel it.

Even what's bad seems laudable because loving has taught me to make good out of everything a little too

Much.

The Aftermath to Death of Time

I guess feeling
Nothing at all
For some time was
A part of feeling
Everything for
The time being.
I guess feeling
Completely
Unloved for some
Time was a part of feeling the
Love for as long as it could last.
I guess I believed
It now, this is
How it goes and I
Hate it. I hate
How it doesn't last long enough
Yet doesn't end.
For the time being even after Time
Itself dies.

Me, A So-Called Stone

Stern

Faceless

Devoid of any emotions

A callous stone

This is what I've become

For you

But what you can't see is

Something so young and

Delicate

Capable of living and

Loving in this disguise of

Forbidding die-hardism

And for once

I want someone to look

Through

And discover how pains

And love dwell together in

Something so emphatic

Yet muted, so human and
Too full of life to be a
Crass stone
I want someone to look
Through me and know me
I'm not austere enough to
Never love
I'm just afraid of breaking.

Irreplaceable Replacements

Replace your heart with me

Let me beat in your chest and keep you

Living

Make me the blood in your veins

Let me flow in your body and scour every

Part of you

You find vile and unholy.

Replace your mind with me

Let me be all you'll ever think about

Let me the skin on your bones

Let me harbor the hurt you haven't hewn

Yet

I won't let there be any fever of sorrow on

You

Let me be the gravity holding your ground

I won't let you fall, fall so hard that such

Delicate like you, breaks.

Replace your sky with me

Let me be all you look up at night

Awake counting the stars, mapping the

Constellations

Replace her with me

Let me be who you love.

The Longing

While my tears hold onto my cheeks and my lips hold onto his name,

My eyes hold onto the starry seven skies up above.

My heart holds onto you, God.

And I wait for us to meet again.

How I Look at Myself

I look at myself , not as a person.

I don't look at myself as you find me.

I see myself as someone you have yet to find.

I look at myself as an unexplored entity, an unseen vision, an unfelt touch.

I find myself too not what you want me to be.

I find myself so dearly in love with everything you've come across.

Even the rage. Even the hate. Even the craze. Even the fate.

Thus I find myself, love.

What They Call Love

You scrape right where it hurts so much.

Exactly where my past lovers lay buried.

Where pangs flow in the corners of my mind, where memories should be silenced.

Where you can't coexist.

You graze those places on my body that still bleed vivaciously.

You hurt every part of me that does not ache for you and call it love.

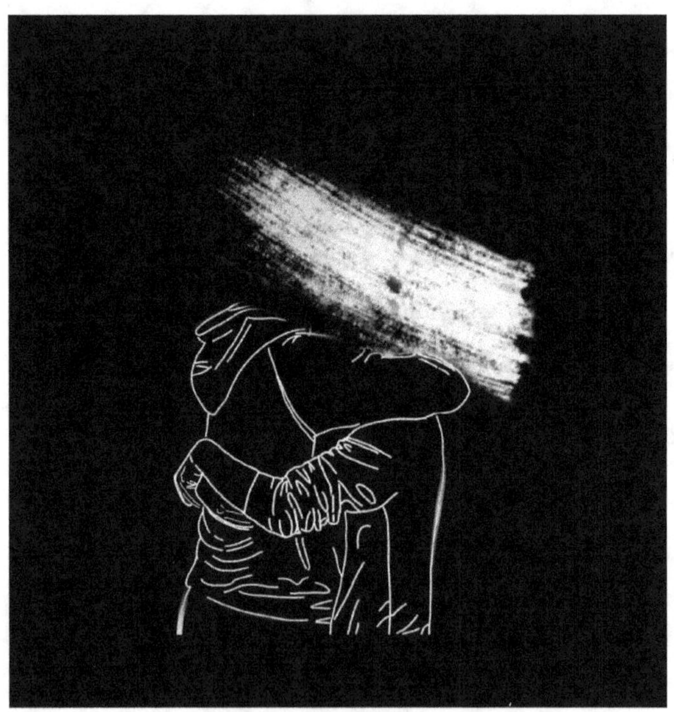

Odd Fads

If you ask me
What kind of fad
Is this
I'd tell you how
People like me love
And make love
Flourish in all
Those places,
You thought
Would be left
Untouched.

How to Love Life

Sometimes, I feel abashed whether I want
Someone who'll understand and help me
Make a difference or someone who just won't
Leave and hold my hand;
Whether I need someone who'll cry with
Me or wipe off my tears and tell me stop
Mourning my past,
Whether I want some arms to catch me when
I fall or somebody who won't let me fall as I
Stumble,
Whether I want somebody to carry my heavy
Heart or just hold my head,
Whether I need a face to gaze at or an
Existence to think about,
Whether I want to feel loved or just let it all
Out,
Whether I want someone to understand or

Somebody to feel

You can understand but you can't feel

While I can feel but not understand.

I guess it's you I've always wanted and needed

Nobody else except my own self.

And I knew before loving my life, I had to learn

To accept it.

Love and other solaces

You are not a

Fool to find

Agony beautiful

It's the time

When you find

Your loved ones

It's the place

Where you look

For solace

It's the person in who you find

Love.

The Artists of Sorrow

I've met a few artists and I've seen it in their eyes.

That miserable urge. That cruel helplessness.

If only they could gather the strength to paint out or draw away the love for their lovers

And the pains of their past. They wouldn't just be artists but clones of happiness.

But sadly, they're nobodys for now. They are nothing but merely some people. Detached from their very existences.

Drugs and Men

It's 09:13 am. He shoves some pills in my coat's pocket during our ride in some fracturing rickshaw today.

I stare at him blankly flustered.

What drugs can do to someone.

Look at their power. Alive. Seated beside me.

Look at their bulging eyes. Look at them bursting to consume every feeling of being that has ever been there.

Hear them breathe.

Hear the weight of them.

The heaviness.

Feel them. Feel their desire. Their very contagiousness.

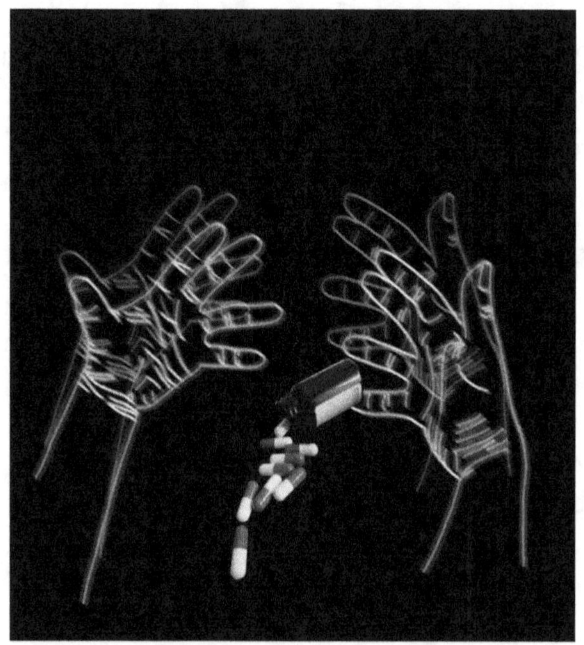

You, My Sky And Me

So far away

There's something celestial

Something too beautiful for my touch

So colossal

I can not embrace

It's endless for my vision

It's the sky

It's you

The day and the night struggle to be within

Your walls while your sun and moon keep

An eye on me and chase me everywhere I

Go on this lifeless orb that is dead only

Without

Your colors

You could be my universe but how could I

Have a universe when even you seem to be

More than enough, more than I could want but need

You could be my world but I have the globe

Of mine that could only be a world with a

Sky like you

Indeed, you're my sky

There with me in the dark

There with me in light

There to bless my eyes

With your lilacs and tangerines as you cradle the sun a sleep to its awakenings

There to cry and thunder as I weep and

Crumble

There on fire when I'm cold

There with the zephyr carrying whiffs of all

The happiness and sorrow when I'm warm

You're there containing the colors when everything seems just about blacks, whites

And grays.

You're something

Not everything

Something without which everything would

Cease to exist.

Love and Other Strangers

I know you're tired of crying to strangers

I know you're tired of explaining how much it hurts

And still nobody understands that the pain is

Getting unbearable. It's not heartbreak, it's hurt. It Just hurts staying awake all night wondering if he's

Sleeping knowing that you're in pain.

It hurts knowing that he doesn't love you you're not

Enough and never will be. You're tired of hoping that

One day maybe one day he'll realize that he loves

You and it's a day that's never going to arrive but you'll

Still text him I love yous and that you'll be waiting with Tears in your eyes.

You've cried too much. You've turned into an ocean

And every tears stays afloat on you and you Drown in your own miseries. (I know you're tired of loving and loving and loving. And You're also tired of hurting and hoping but Still carrying on clear in everything blurry.

I know you're tired of waiting and I know

You're tired of being tired. I know tired

Doesn't seem to be the right word for how
You feel because it's much more than
Hurting and tiring.
I know it's getting too much but someone will
Love you, love the way you don't give up and still
Whisper the name of your beloved while crying a
River and owning two wrists bleeding hopelessly. I
Know it's too much for you and I'm not going to lie
That it's all going to be alright but you'll be
Loved. Someone will love you.)

You, A Succumbed Star

I was such a fool
To ever think you
Left the sky, the
Glooms and Auroras to just meet me here.
What I should've
Known was that you were just a succumbed
Star.
Shattering.
For that love.
To be wished upon by someone better
Somewhere else.

How To Not Move On

But the truth is that there is no moving on

It's just carrying on

There is no letting go

We're just trying to let in more

Someone else in the name of love

There are no two apart

When one is sharing his heart

There is no forever in your never

Love can never be played a game so clever

There might be some heartbreaking

But some people are worth the risks we're taking

So fall in love, adore, be miserable but please do love

It's hard to believe

How you'll never leave it

All you can do is heave it.

Love and Other Defeats

And I know one day
I just won't be able to sugar-coat this
Bitter pain in the name of love
With pretty words strangled between
Some lines on tons of pages
With "I still love you" crouched on my
Tongue since the last moment I felt you
Nigher
With my eyes staring into the dead air,
Unconsciously seeking your deep
Brown eyes to get lost into
With my cold hands yearning for the warmth of yours,
Restless feet waiting to run into you
With this soul aching for your healing
With this heart shattering to harmonize
With yours
I just won't be able to survive it for long
But I'll be able to love
I'd still be in love
With you.

Butterflies, A Prey to Fate

Love has a disparate way of making you

Feel alive

You'll feel from caterpillars crawling

Inside your ribcage and settling in your

Heart to butterflies tickling your guts

Until they fall a prey to fate

Until fate kills every little thing keeping

You alive or leave those butterflies

Breathing their last

Until fate decides

You must not encage these emotions,

These entities inside you for so long

But let them out

Let them all out

Let them go

For this kismet then decides

They no longer belong there

They belong outside

Into the wilderness but your insides
And that's how love makes life disparate
It makes you alive when you love
It gives you birth when you let go
To love on, to live on
With nothing encaged and nudged but
Free and uncluttered.

Finding Yourself

That's the most beautiful thing about love,
You'd find yourself,
You'd have yourself, You'd give yourself, You'd be,
with, someone else.
Then.
You'd become yourself.
Love makes you, yourself, in the end.
Because this is all what you're about, love
Becoming yourself.

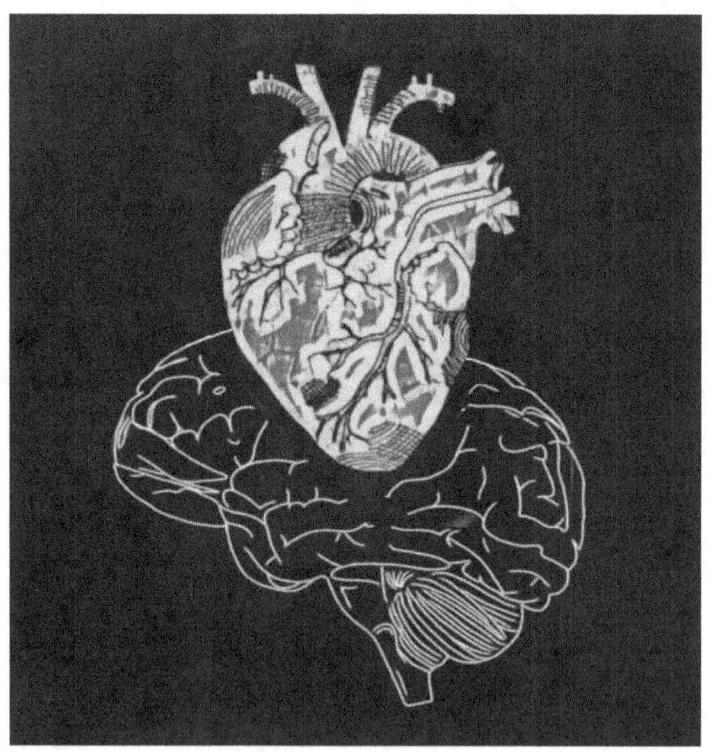

You and Your Words

Your words are veiled with lively gaiety But when I try to look through the space between the clotted words shoved out of your lips

I find you stuck in moments you had

Surrendered to hope and love but drove

Yourself afar from it yet memorized the

Maps to this agonizing nostalgia

For maybe it'd be good to visit it once again

Maybe it'll be good to feel what you never

Wanted yet it's something you needed, you

Do

And when I see you

I find your beaming face above the soul

Melting in the fire set ablaze by what is too intense to be blazoned on words, silence and your entire being. It's just there unseen, unheard, untouched, unfelt yet.

Cigarettes and Us

We are like ashes.
Remains of burnt
Cigarettes.
And we can't
Reckon when we'll
Drift away with
Time.
Drift away into
Nothingness.
Unless we're
Suffering from
Unrequited love.
Kept in an
Ashtray but
Unprivileged to
Scorch.
But weren't we
Murdered the
Moment we were
Set on fire.

Things We Wait for, After Death

We're mere lifeless vessels walking around pretending we can love, we feel.

You're just another puppet and I'm just

Some skin and bones hoping we'd be loved, We're talking like no better melodies can build homes in hearts and words like honey We starve for and those we spill.

I scratch my skin off and you break your

Strings and we fall, we fall and we fall

Deeper and deeper in this void we call love.

We're still lifeless vessels waiting to come

Alive and be filled with love and affection when all we'll be is empty waiting someone to caress us back to life. We'll still be dead

Waiting for love

Waiting in love

Waiting to love.

Absurd Denials

I write about you

And it's futile

Denying that

Because life's

Too short to hide

And live in

Denial

But it's also

Useless to admit

That there are no words to describe my love for you

That's completely

Possible

Unless you're in

Denial too that You don't love me don't

Be in

Doubts and denial

When you're in

Love, it'll ruin

You.

Lies, if They Lasted

And finally she realized

My love is true

Because lies don't last long.

Things That I Envy the Most

I envy the air

You breathe

I envy the tears

You cry

I envy the smiles

You wear

I envy the scent

Of your cologne

I envy the

Cigarettes you

Smoke

I envy the eyes

Gazing at you

I envy the lips

You kiss

I envy the hands

You hold

I envy the ground

You walk on

I envy the skin

On your bones

I envy the heart

In your chest

I envy the way they're so close to you.

And I'm just not.

I'm too far away.

Things That I'd do if I Could

If I could

I'd hold the universe still

Until our fate prevails upon you in

Love with me

If I could

I'd curtail the horizon to have you

Next to me

If I could

I'd turn the worlds upside down just

For our trails to be one

If I could

I'd cross hades for your heaven

If I could

I'd make you mine

If I could

I'd make forever exist

If I could

I would've done it by now.

Sadness

You know that's the thing about

Sadness that no matter what it's always

There. It doesn't matter how many anti-

Depressants I take, I have this

Melancholy inside me all the time. I

Wake up at night wanting to scream

And cry myself to sleep. It's always

There even when I'm happy. It reminds

Me how I won't be able to wear that

Smile for long. Now that I come to think

Of it, happiness is all history and

Sadness is all I have. Dolor is all I have

To embrace when I'm alone, hopeless

And lost. No matter what it's always

Going to be there even when I'm surrounded by laughter.
That's why

Poets preach sadness because they

Know grief will stay, not because they

Don't know the taste of real
Happiness. But because they know how
To heave a heavy heart and just remain
Silent with words crowded in their heads.

I Love and I'm not in Love

You heard the word "love" from my mouth

Again

I confessed for the 107th time now.

You tighten your fist out of rage while your

Eyes are bulging and your teeth jitter against

Each other but that's what you want me to see. You hate this word it's so hard to reckon.

So hard to fathom.

But I see beyond. I rhapsodize what I want to see.

I want to see how much you've hurt. I want to

See how much you're in pain. I want to see how cruelly Someone poisoned your love with pain. I want to see it in the rage. I want

To see it in this monster, you think you are.

I want to stare at this moth allured to his

Death. I want to see what she made you. I

Want to see someone you've been afraid of

Becoming. I want to see what you're becoming. And I'm going to be there to see. I'm going to stay. I'm going to be here at your worst. And I can't wait to see you. So I can hold you and tell you I see you. I love you.

She just looked at you.

She was just in love.

And I'm not her.

Unfortunately, I'm not her;

Mother

Mother
Neither do I know
How it felt when
You held me in Your arms for the First time nor
When you tucked
My hair, on my
Forehead, behind
My ear on my
First day of
School
But I remember
The grimace you
Wore on your face
When I told you I
Sprained my ankle
And I don't
Remember how old
I was

And I remember

The grin spread

Across your face

When I got my first

Periods and

Thought I was

Going to die

And now that you

Are sitting

Beside me with

Your hand resting

On my shoulder

The world seems

To stop spinning

Like there's not

A wonder such as

You and indeed

You are more

Beautiful than

The word

Mother.

Me before you

I've heard, you can't love someone until you don't love yourself and I've hated myself to bear these words. We Don't choose to wake up the love on

Our own. We don't face it. We let it

Happen as it happens. We victimize ourselves may be to learn how to love ourselves.

I've never believed in self love. I've

Known a feeling instead that arises sometimes even when you're on the

Verge of killing yourself by hatred when you learn to empathize love, you learn to love by bits to inches to a whole. You simply fathom to appreciate

Yourself when you give love. You begin

To admire yourself for how at times

You may not be able to love yourself

Yet you love. You love the hardest. You

Give love to the fullest to those who are

Not even close to you. To being you ,

To being yours.

Heart Breakers

What broke me the most

Lost hopes,

Wasted love,

Cold goodbyes,

And then there

Was you,

Who broke me the most.

Love for the Selfish

We say we love

Each other

When all you want

Is someone to

Preach you

And that's not how love is, it doesn't hurt that

Much.

For

May be,

Sometimes your

Love is not enough

To make someone

Stay or it's too much to let them go.

Love, a Panacea

You've doped me with this panacea I never knew

I could devour.

I urged for hurt and love that dose

Everything but heal because it seemed like It was the best I could have and, whatever elixir you've doped me with, I don't want it to wear off this lucky time.

For you,

It is making me feel everything that i thought wasn't there to be felt.

Is this real

If it isn't, I still want it.

Loving in Serene Skies and Stormy Nights

No, it's not me missing you once again

It's the starry sky, this dark night

It's that every star I see looking out for you

It's the moon eying you while you lie beside

The thought of loving her

These are the clouds that don't tend to

Reside by the notion of being nostalgic for

All those memories never made

It's everything around me singing the blues

In your longing

And I

I am just loving you from the horizon

The waves, the tides, of all the oceans and seas in parts known and unknown of this world.

Kicking around somewhere.

They fall and rise. They too are inevitably in love with you. You my moon. Of my serene sky and

Even my stormy nights.

Infatuations

We say we're not going to fall for each other

We are not going to fall in love but we are such fools

We'll still call each other incessantly for no fucking

Reason but I won't hang up because you say you want

To hear me breaths since I can't talk

I'm busy romanticizing myself with someone else

We don't love

We won't love

But you'll ask me every damn day how I'm looking

And I'll ask you every fucking hour if you're busy

We're just friends

We're just bold

We just talk how it feel likes to be in love, the

Pleasures of it, the pains of it

But still, we want to touch our hands and feel

Awkward about it

And you never even want to talk

You just want me welded to you

You ask me about myself what even I don't know

And I tell you to find out

And when you ask me

What are we

Then we're just like

We are not in love

Then what are we I ask myself

We are just in denial

My heart tells yours

We are just not ready to accept

That after hurting so much over a love

How can we love again and not hurt as much as we

Did before

We are unfortunately in something like it again

Infatuation whatever I guess

But just somehow tortuous and getting away with the

Nearing heartache.

Hand in hand

Hold my hands

Hold my hands

When they'll be numb and cold

Hold my hands

When the space between those fingers will be

Just dead air

Hold my hands

When the life in them will be austere

Hold my hands

Hold my hands

When the skin is iced and quiet

Hold my hands

Even when it's too late

Just hold my hands

Even when the warmth of yours won't be enough

Hold my hands

Hold my hands

When they're implanted in the soil

Hold my hands.

When they're wrapped in the petrichor and

Softened in some mud

Hold my hands

When they turn to dust

Hold my hands

Just hold my hands

Hold my hands with yours.

You and I Both

You and I

Are akin through

Some pains

Before any

Kismet or karma

So

What is the

Love

They talk so

Much about

So highly of yet

Belittle

Everything you've done, undone, and not done so far

Everything you've said aloud like an

Explosion and left unsaid silently like

Air in a vacuum

Everything you've romanticized even

When you're agonized

Everything you've endured, you've

Been miserable, you've been happier

Every tear, every pain you have

Allowed to parch

Every atom you've poeticized for it

For this word called love

Don't tell me just a feeling

Don't tell me just a mere feeling can

Make so much happen

How can you just shrink all these

Happenings and unhappenings in

Just a feeling

No, love is not just a feeling

It's a lot more.

More than any words can describe or some art can portray.
More than I can exaggerate or

Amplify.

The Pursuits of Love

And the world somehow found ways to tear

Us apart

Behind that frontal of chutzpah, I failed to

Trespass these galaxies in between

Instead I decided to die every day in this

Iniquity

To meliorate something that was never torn

Nor broken, I felt the need to cashier meteors

Of words with comets of intimations instead of shedding tears and keening. All I could feel was agonizing myself and you before the pursuits of love.

All I could ever do was decay after my

Infirmity."

Love As We Call It

It's been weeks since we haven't been

In contact. We haven't blathered in person or on the

Phone. And I don't want to ask awfully how are You.

I want to know, ask you instead if your skin is warm

Like the depression in a couch is after someone has

Sat in it for too long. Are your eyes easy like the sky is

When a new day is dawning. Tell me you didn't brush

Your hair with your hands instead of the comb, In front

Of that tall mirror in your room, which hasn't been

Displaced an inch for as far as I can remember. Do

Your hands still smell like a fucking toothpaste

Because of your favorite mint soap. Does

your voice still get hale and loud when you're happy As if
you had won a hopeless argument every

Time. Have you touched any of those poetry books,

You keep stacking up. Do all the heartbreak songs still

Fascinate you and seem horribly addictive. Do you

Still walk like you're going to stumble and fall any

Second and sit like you own the place that bears you.
Have you changed your useless rose colored lip balm
Or do you still complain about your chapped lips. Do
You still laugh hysterically at stupid jokes while trying
To hide your uneven teeth. Do you still carry on eating
While mumbling that you can't have anymore. Do you
Still demand your cardamom tea to be as dark as
Your sense of hum our and the amount of sweetness
Not to be questioned. Do you still think Paul walker is
Alive somewhere, waiting for you to find him so you
Both can get married. And I want to ask everything you
Found so trifling to put heads together fro. But what I
Really want to know is if you're still the same. The
Same angel I fell in love with. I want to know if you're
Back to being you, after I messed up. Before I
Unintentionally recklessly made you feel unlovable.

Eyes, Oceans in the Human Body

I know how arduous it is to have oceans contained behind your eyes and you can't even disburden a drop.

You just can't make a few tears spurt out of between your eyelids

I know it's so painful.

I know but endure it because that's what humans are for.

Mere Moments

Then there comes a moment
When you realize you really
Have no body.
There comes the moment
When you can't keep yourself
Together anymore.
There comes the moment
When time doesn't matter.
There comes the moment
You lose yourself.
There comes the moment
When you find yourself still in
Love with the person you
Thought you had let gone.
There comes the moment
When you still care about what
You'd never should.
There comes the moment

When you realize

No one is going to

Be there but you

Watering down

Some moonshine

In a heavy glass

While staring into

The numb air

Again

Because darling, you loved him

You loved him so much

No one could ever love that way

And you're not apart for that way

You're apart for the way you

Didn't

You're apart and unfathomable

Because you loved

In a world, where people have

Forgotten how it feels

They could never descry it like

You do.

To the People You Call Your Universe

There is a thing about this universe

At times it can condense into an entity

In all likelihood

A small speck of dust but human

And at times it can run out of sight just like that

Disappear right in front of one's eyes too weak to

Catch sight of something so colossal in hours,

Days, weeks, maybe decades

Because

It's a person

Holding a universe within

Constellation on his skin

Galaxies bursting in his lungs

A person

A so called speck of dust in nothingness

A universe in not so many

A person

You just couldn't get a hold of

So celestial to it's core

For one's hand are covered in nothing but way

Too many sins

A person

You love to find out they are nothing alike the

World you exist in they're possibly everything the

World strives for

You love to fathom there are greater words you haven't discovered yet to poeticize him

You love to realize there is no such poem to

Contain someone so prodigious.

And in that moment

You'll ask yourself

Who have you come so far

For

And you won't be able to say

Your own name but his

You'll call his name

Unfortunately, this is exactly

What you'll do

You'll envision him

Unknowingly, why.

Love and Other Songs

Ever heard any song so beautiful

You feel yourself floating on the melody

And at times, drowning in the lyrics

Trying to get a hold of the rhythm

Suffocated but somewhat alive

You, you're that song.

To Love and to Let Go

There's so much to be with and without

And here I am in this nature with a God,

Among some destinies and desires

Granting to be with and

Refusing partly or utterly without you

There's so much, so damn much

To love and to let go. And here I am choosing you above all else.

Whether it be loving or letting go.

Whether it be my destiny or my desire

Whether it becomes me with or without you.

You, My World

If I told you

I saw you in the

Sky today

You wouldn't

Know

You wouldn't

Believe

You don't see

You how I see

You

I see a world

Full of you

A world I call

My own.

Mirrors That Lie

I'm not going to stare into this enticing

But deluding mirror today

I just won't

Instead I'm going to run my hands in my hair like

Frosted thread sutured to my scalp

I'm going to let my finger tips feel the pores in my

Skin like shallow minute tunnels

I'm going to be lost in the sphinxes of my finger prints

And dance on the lines of my palms

I'm going to close my eyes and my eyes to the

Beauty I keep within and spread across my bones protruding

Out of my skin

I'm going to feel the warms and colds of it

Feel the colors of my façade that fade into another With the diverse lights and murk at odds I'm going to do fair to what has been told to be changed

I'm going to adorn or undress what suits my heart, my

Dignity

I'm going to explore my vessel with my ace eyes and

Hands

I'm going to find perfection in the skewness of my

Body

Even the places I can't lay my eyes on and make my

Hands visit easily

But what I can

I'm going to brush my eyelashes with my forefinger

And fondle them meeting as I close my eyelids

And let those eyes settle in their mettle

I'm going to unfurl my uneven teeth in front of my

Fears and insecurities as I ask them

If they can define beauty like my flaws just did

I'm going to love every unconscious detail of me

Love it all the way it is

I am going to be faithful to me

Instead of relying on a mere mirror

That shows me less than a whole

That highlights the flaws which my delicacy can tuck

Away in a blink

I won't see the mirror

I'd rather see me

And I'd love myself for all the mirrors are the same

But I live among differences and my eyes are forever
Going to be my own

No reflection or another's perusal can define me but

Me

Along with the fabric that conceals the inches of my

Skin isn't capable of laying my purity bare

It's me

My essence under the wraps of my conscience

And such art like me

Only deserves to be cosseted and fancied This is my worth
This is a human's worth, Human so beautiful as you.

You and Your Words pt 2

Your words made

Me feel something

Maybe they made

Me love you

Maybe they made

You hurt me

But at least they

Were yours

No matter how

Hard they made me

Feel

Anything you'll

Ever give is

Copacetic even if

It's just hurt.

Love and Other Odysseys

Maybe loving is just running,

Running and more running.

With no destination to this

Odyssey. But for a destiny

Not so lonely.

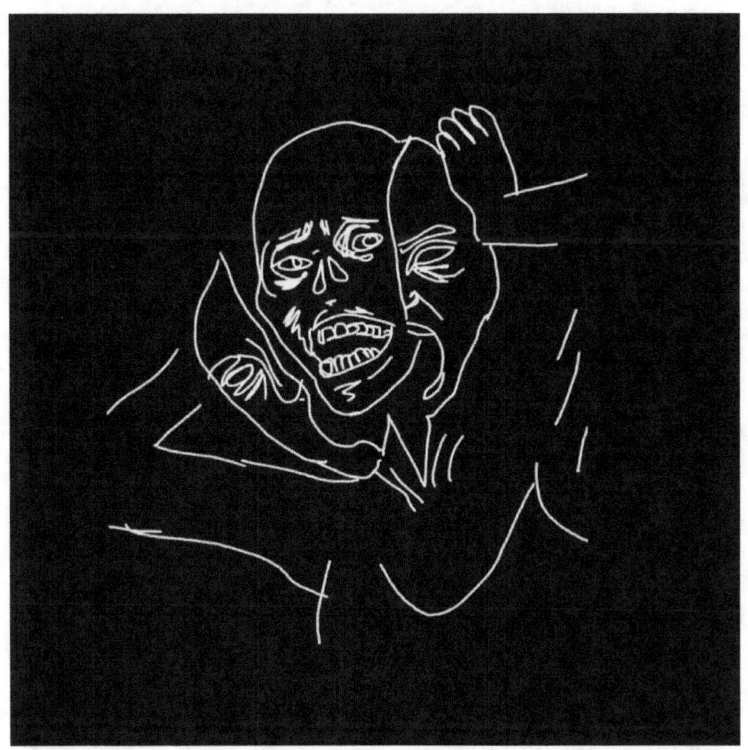

Love Before Habits

Someone once asked me if I

Really loved or had I just made

Habits out of some people. So I

Left them all and it me.

Of course, I loved because I

Always could. I loved because I

Always could. I loved because if I could make habits out of them, we don't miss habits, we miss love.

then certainly, I could

Find love among them. If I could

Find them worth making a habit

Out of them. I can love them. I can hurt for them, I can love because there is always more to a person than his self but love and forevers.

Our Breaths

Now my breaths stink like yours.

It stenches of too many cigarettes rumpled in a warm ashtray.

Too much of that vivid liquor, staining my creased lips.

Too much of trying to forget,

Being crazy in love with something I can't drink or smoke.

Something I just can't take enough of.

Someone I can't have.

What to Tell the Lovers and the Beloved

Tell all the lovers
Their love is in vain
They've loved wrong.

Tell all the
beloved
They deserve no love.
There exists not the right love

Tell all the lovers
There is no right person for them to
Be with
There is no right place for them to
Breathe.

Tell all the beloved
Love occurs with time
Love looks for the right ones

Love fades beyond the horizon.

Then come to me

Tell me

Do I be the lover or the beloved.

What Lies Interstellar

Maybe the sun craves the darkness.

Maybe the moon is just

Unwittingly in love with this world.

Or maybe love exists in

Some hearts or some realm,

In some cosmos, we've never believed in.

And all of it lies interstellar.

What I don't Know About Myself

I know

I've become bitter like the chill of the night

I still seem bitter in the honeyed daylight

I know my eyes now look cold like the brittle dead

Leaves of the autumn

I know

I've become quite like my unhealed scars that are

Suffocating under my sleeves , yet won't bellow for an

Ounce of some salve

I know I'm a lot more toxic than the venom in my

Words

I know I'm a lot more cold than with the whatever

In me, is dead

I know I'm a lot more quiet than the vacuum in my

Soul

And I don't know if there's an antitoxin to the venom I

Run

I don't know if this bitterness can be sugared

I don't know if there's a fiery sun to be this cold

I don't know if this winter can be warm

I don't know if there are tolerable words to my silence I don't know if my voice can have that grace it had.

I know there is a lot I don't know

But what I really want to know is if I'll ever be able to

Love with a heart I loved once.

There but not Here

I might not be there to love you but I'm
Here
I might not be there staring into your eyes drowning in
Your blues, but I'm here
I might not be there to caress your scars every
Second your past haunts you but I'm here
I might not be there to choke on every puff of your
Cigarette that you light up when you're burning in grief
But I'm here
I might not be there to taste the wine absorbed in
Your lips, Knowing I hate the fact that you drink too
Heavy and throw up before passing out on the
Floor but I'm here
I might not be there to seize the cold blade,
You often have it sitting on your wrist while deciding
Whether you should end yourself right then or not but
I'm here
I might not be there when you're bawling your eyes
Out wanting for someone to hold you in your arms so

badly but I'm here

I might not be there when you're silently staring at the

Leaden sky, letting the sun blind but I'm here

I might not be there when you're trying to fall asleep,

Afraid you'll have the same nightmares again, but I'm

Here

I might not be there when you're boring your eyes into

The mirror, finding every loathsome detail of you but I'm
here

I'm here when life seems to be so unfair

I'm here when you have no one to feel the pain you

Carry, feel everything you've been holding within for

So long

I'm here ready to have my body carved the way you

Want it to be instead of having you gash your

Precious skin with a piece of a hopeless metal

I'm here to listen to the tragedies behind your every

Scar

I'm here to drink your pain

I'm here to batter every toxic cigarette you'll allow

Close to your lips

I'm here to give an audience to your silence

I'm here to make you realize the eyes of the world lie,

The mirrors lie, but my eyes

They see your delicacy, they see the beauty in you

I'm here to spread my arms around your soul and

Beatify it with all the love even the entire universe

Would fail to give

I'm here with no ambit between us

I'm here to love you

Love you more than anyone can

You might be out of touch but you know I'll never be out
of reach.

Plethora of love

You put so much love into a person

You shouldn't have emptied yourself

Completely

But you did it right

When you've never been empty

How would you know

You were replete once

So empty yourself often

You'll eventually be plethoric

Perhaps

Enough.

To Those who Promise Forevers

Don't promise me any forevers

Just promise me

You'll make it worth it your wanting while

Promise me you might break me

But you'll teach me love

You'll render me the patience of pain

You'll enlighten me with the beauty of brokenness

You'll implant me in the dirts of healing

Promise me

You'll love

Promise me

You'll do it for me

Promise me

You'll love me

- (Why do these eyes fall in love more with what they can't see.)

Blue Butterflies not by Charles Bukowski

There are blue butterflies in my lungs

They won't let me sit and breathe

They won't cut and run my skin

They won't bolt out of my mouth

While I whisper them a desperate goodbye

I say I don't want to inhale

Intoxicants to kill you

I want you to live yellow elsewhere

There are blue butterflies in my guts that won't let my soul rest beside my spine

They won't let me eat pain and drink some hope without aching my insides

They won't cut and run my skin

They won't surge out my veins or rush out of my ears, gush between my lips

I say do you want me to cut supplies to your hopes and my pains

There are blue butterflies probing, reading, my palms

They won't stop telling me my misfortunes

They won't stop reminding me of the very old fading lines
as I olden every damn day

They won't cut and run my skin

They won't rush from between my fingers before I fist my
hands obliging them a leave

I say do you want me to scour my palms shrivelled clean
for the palmist in my hometown could no longer earn

There are blue butterflies tickling my feet cold in the
middle of the night I curl my toes entwining them with a
blanket not cold enough to warm these butterflies

I wake up not slept in the shadow of these butterflies

They won't let me touch the ground

Their wings too cuspate for my fragile shell

They won't cut and run my skin

They won't leave me alone when everyone does

And I doubt I'm so lovesome

Why so, do they do it

I don't know and these blue butterflies won't tell.

The Greatest Myth of Love

If I were to love

I'd love a love

Romeo and Juliet could conquer their kin and let

Alone their deaths

A love, the death of which Anthony won't believe

A love, no snake could taste and for no Cleopatra

Would have to die

A better love than Orpheus, who couldn't rip his

Eyes out for awhile just to have his love with him

For a little longer

A love that let's Scarlett tomorrow not be just

Any other day to obey love

A loco love Layla and majnun, the would dare

Couldn't refuse to see thrive

A love gianciotto would die himself to have

A love isolde won't color the sails with

And a love that you wouldn't refuse to love Because I've
just made myself believe my love is

Greater than any myths on love.

Love and Other Memories

Love that seems to be beckoning goodbye

I'm still holding onto those wilting

Memories of us & those fleeting moments seem to

Be fading again but I'm still loving

I still know how to love

Your worth every time you excite me as

Much as poetry does. You're walking away once

Again but I'm still standing here. I don't want to let go

Off every kiss we've shared, my embrace is still not Ready
to depart. I want to stay in pain besides that Love that
seems to be beckoning goodbye.

I'm still holding onto everything you've left and that's Me.
I'm still holding onto myself. I'm carrying myself

Across the street of incompetence. I'm still sailing in

The oceans of restlessness & reaching the calm shore

Alive but miserable. This is all love had me like. It's all
About the pain & euphoria rousing every inch of me.

I'm still holding onto that blade in my hand because

Sometimes the hurt gets too much, must to be let

Out. It's the kind of hurt I can't scream & cry away. It's

The kind of hurt, only you know the remedy and how

Badly I wish you were here for me to make it easier to

Breathe since each breath has your name

Tattooed on it and it's just hard to conceal it with

Numbness & the voids hold within

They're empty but seem to be red and

Blue because of you, they're tangerine like the autumn

Leaves when I'm falling & ebbing. I' m contriving

Constellations of adoration on this rough surface

Where I have fallen with whisks of words that I can't

Even lift properly

I'm still holding onto those moments when I'm not
Supposed to be getting lost in your eyes. The way I

Watch them sparkle. I'm trying not to hold onto this

Beauty but it's all there is. There's too much of it. It's
Everywhere. On your lips. On your skin. In the color of
Your eyes, the dust on the strands of your hair.

I'm still holding onto the way you walk away and look

Back to know if I'm still standing there waiting for you

To run back Into my arms or have I faded into the love

You're leaving behind. I'm right there where you look

Away hoping that I'd just be a blur, not something worth
seeing or maybe someone too exquisite to be seen by eyes
like your own.

The Writer

A writer won't only give you his heart

He'll write on you

Like on paper

He'll write with his emotions like with a

Pen

He'll give you words

Like a pen does to paper

He'll ink you with his pen

Like one loves with one's heart.

No Fortunes to Tell

I want to tell you something.

But my voice is not loud enough for you to draw.

And my words are thinner than

The air you breathe.

I guess I have no luck for you to love what I have to tell. Because I'm too unfortunate to own even a little of your love.

And maybe if I did have any Luck, I wouldn't have to tell you anything.

Anything such, I find so must.

So moments.

To make you love me.

Anything louder. Anything heavier. Anything enough.

Don't Ask Me

Don't ask me at night

Why am I awake

Ask the moon

Why in the night

Did she choose to stay

Don't ask me why I wish

On falling stars

Ask the stars

Why flaring they fall for

You from so far

Don't ask me what I'm

Staring in the dark

 Ask the dark

Why does it always

Leave me seeking a

Serene spark.

How to be Able of Love

She says

He loves you a lot

It's just that men don't love the same as us

They have a different heart or you can say

They don't express love as we want maybe

Because it's their weakness

I look at my mother's tired swollen eyes,

Her tensed forehead, dead lips and skin, melting

Down her face

And think to myself how absurd it is

Why are our bodies bruised and hurting

As we spread our hands in front of him for

Some bread and some clothes to hide our

True presence

How does he feel uncaged but not mindful

With having things exactly the way he

Wants unlike us

Suffocating sitting and taking all of the hell he gives

How does he act the victim when he

Shoots words like bullets that wound us

How can he be at peace when a drifter lays his

Eyes on us

What kind of love is this I bother her again

She turns her back on me

As if she's telling me I will never have the

Same love I give, I feel

And then I realize it's no longer about his

Love or mine or anyone else's

It's about the pain of not knowing what real

Love is like

How to feel

How to recognize it

How to own it

How to be able of it.